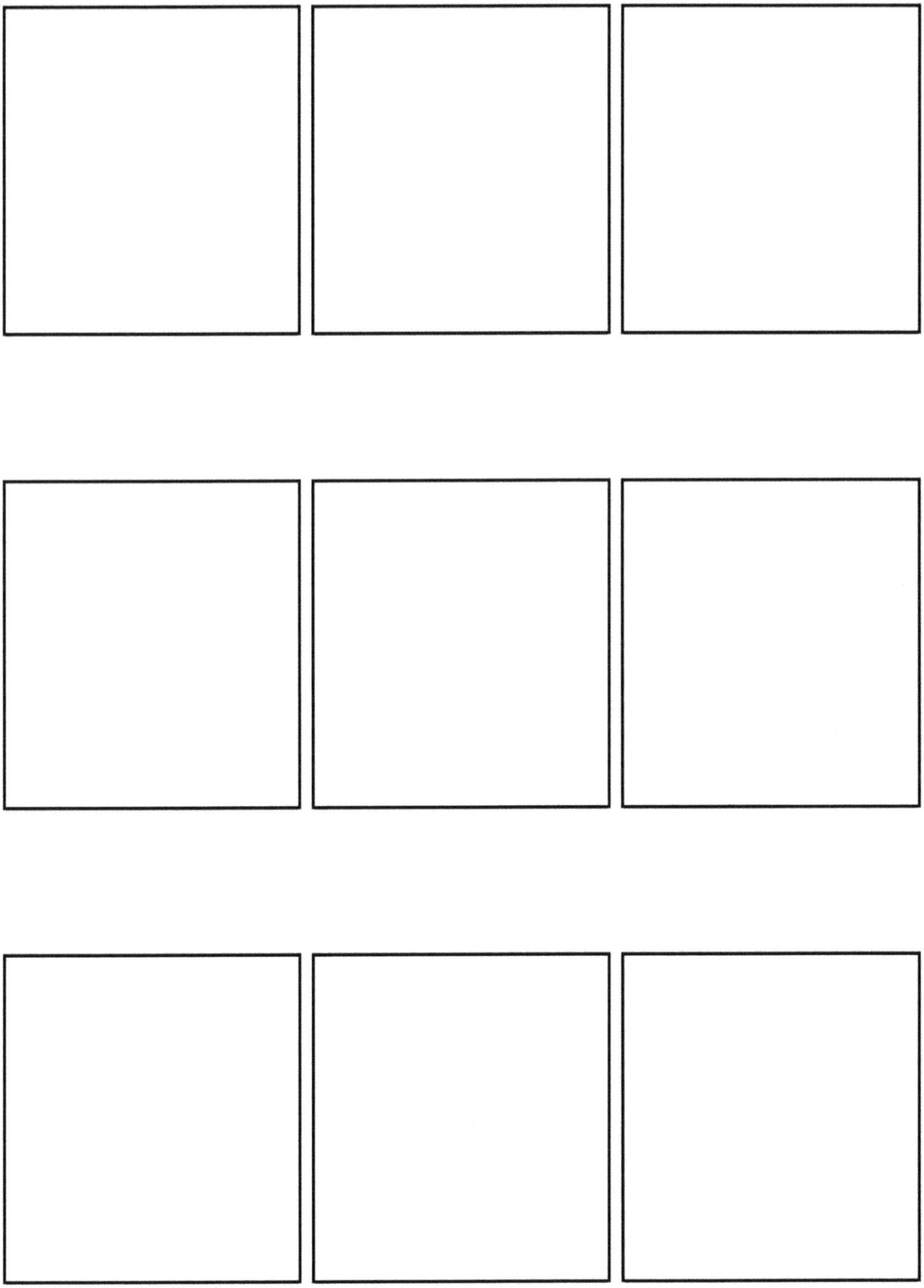

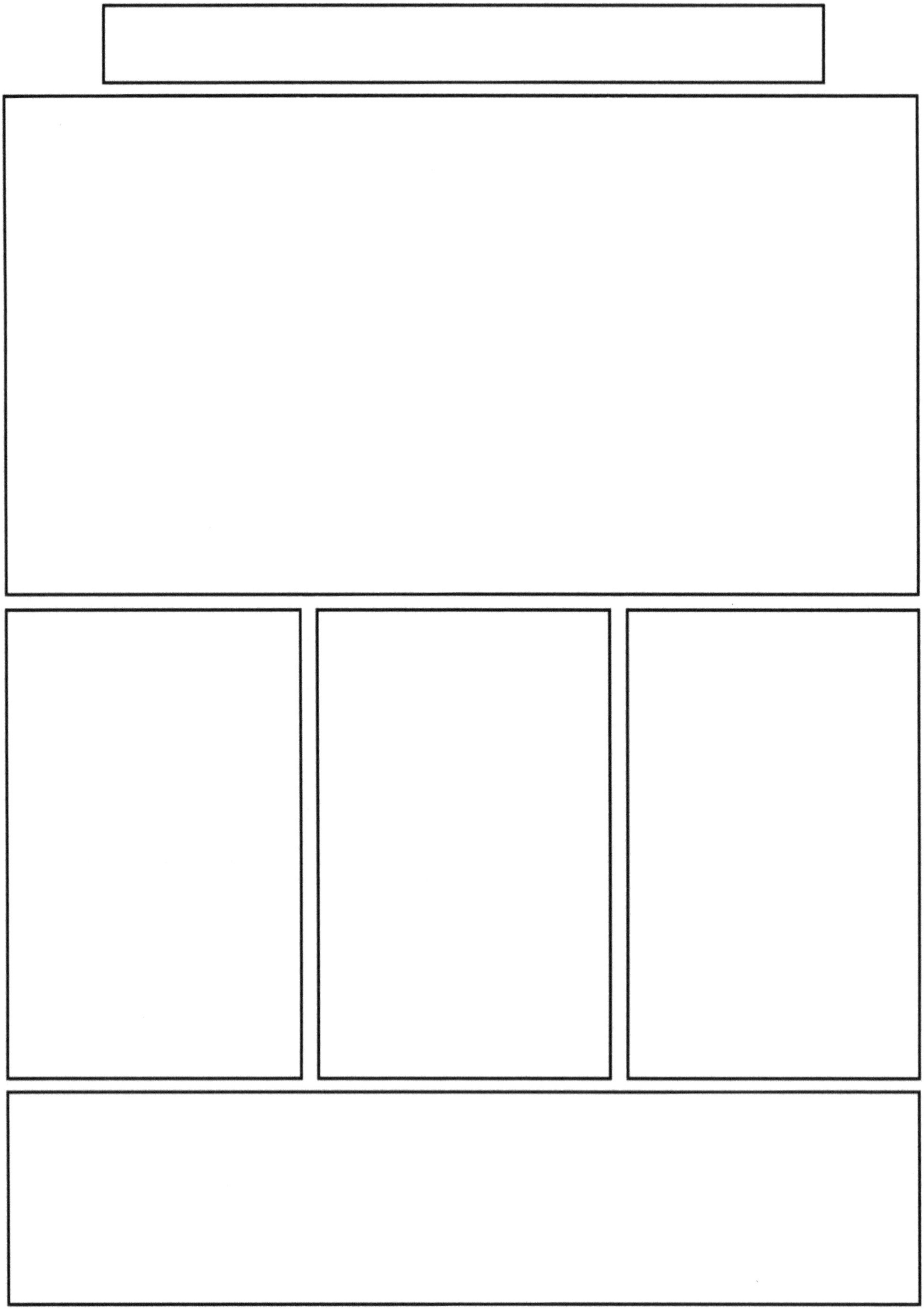

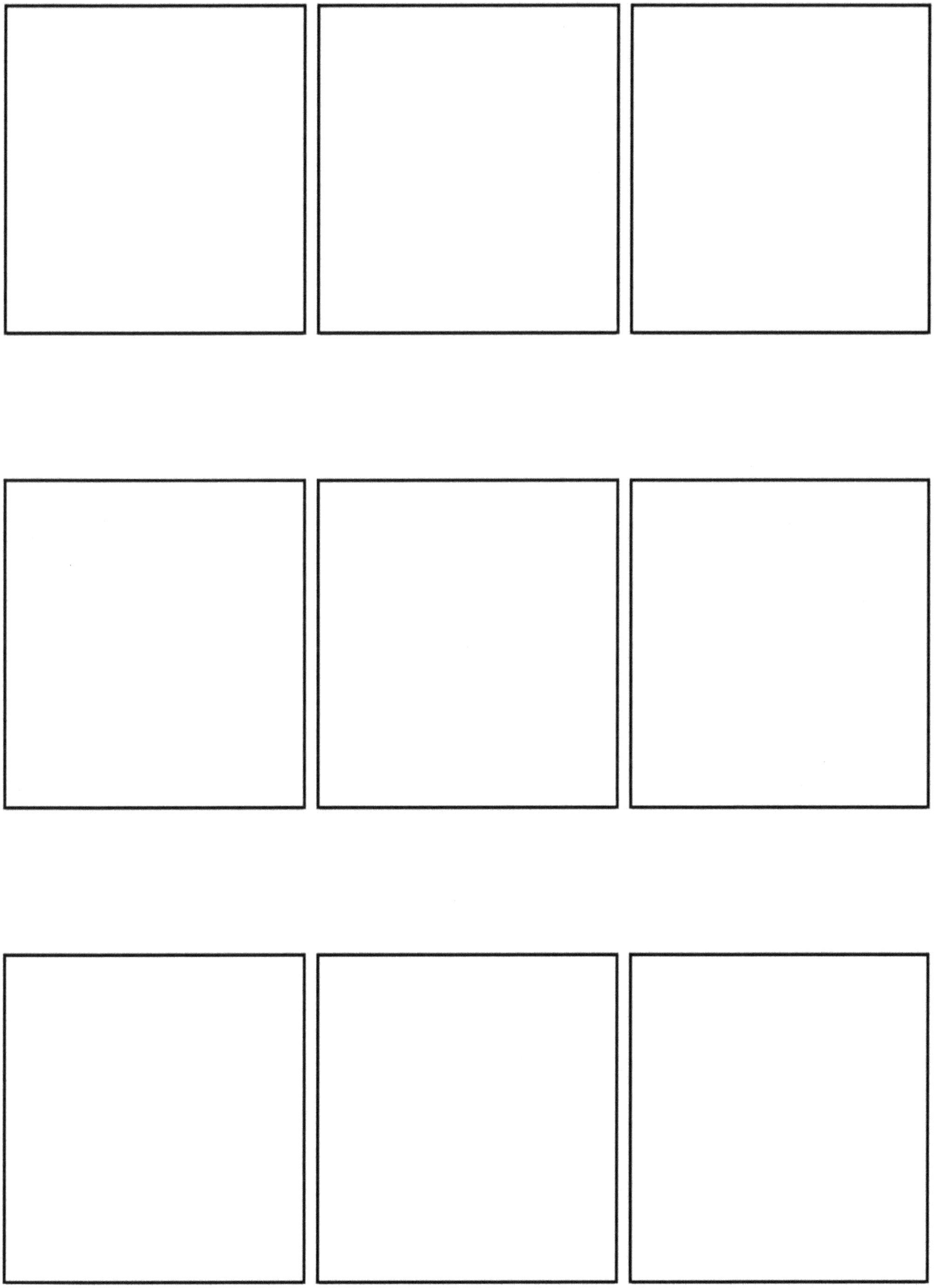

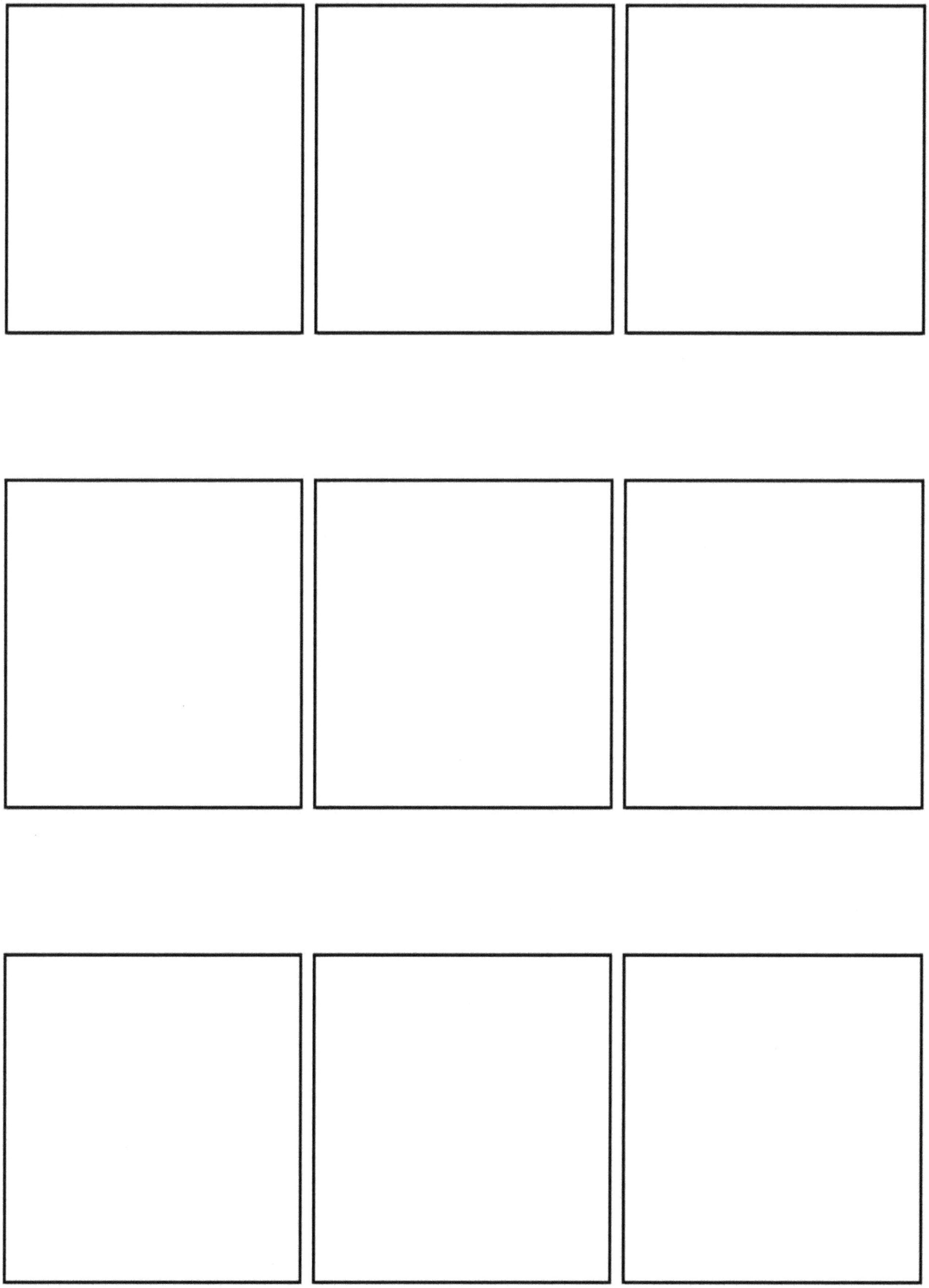

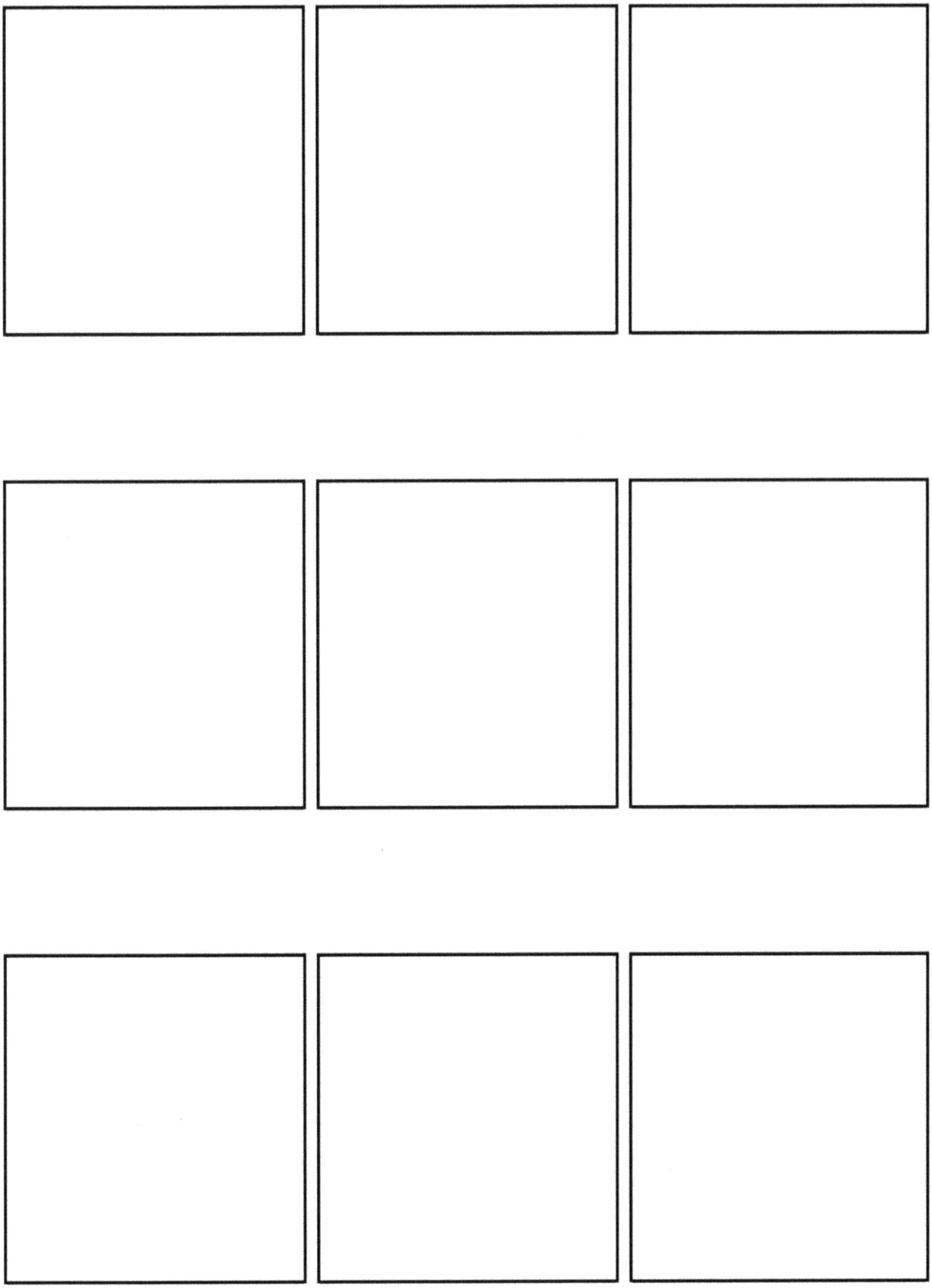

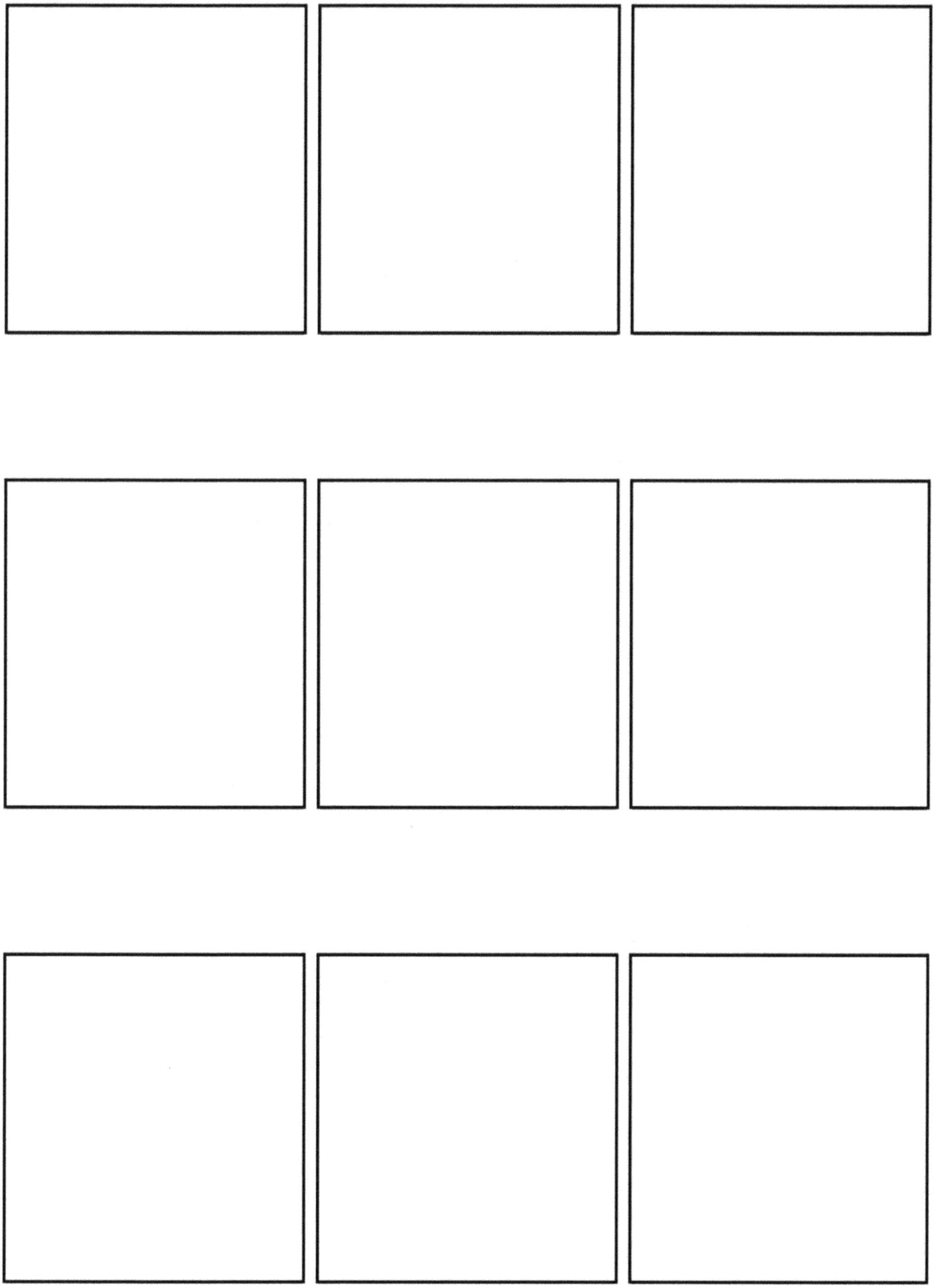

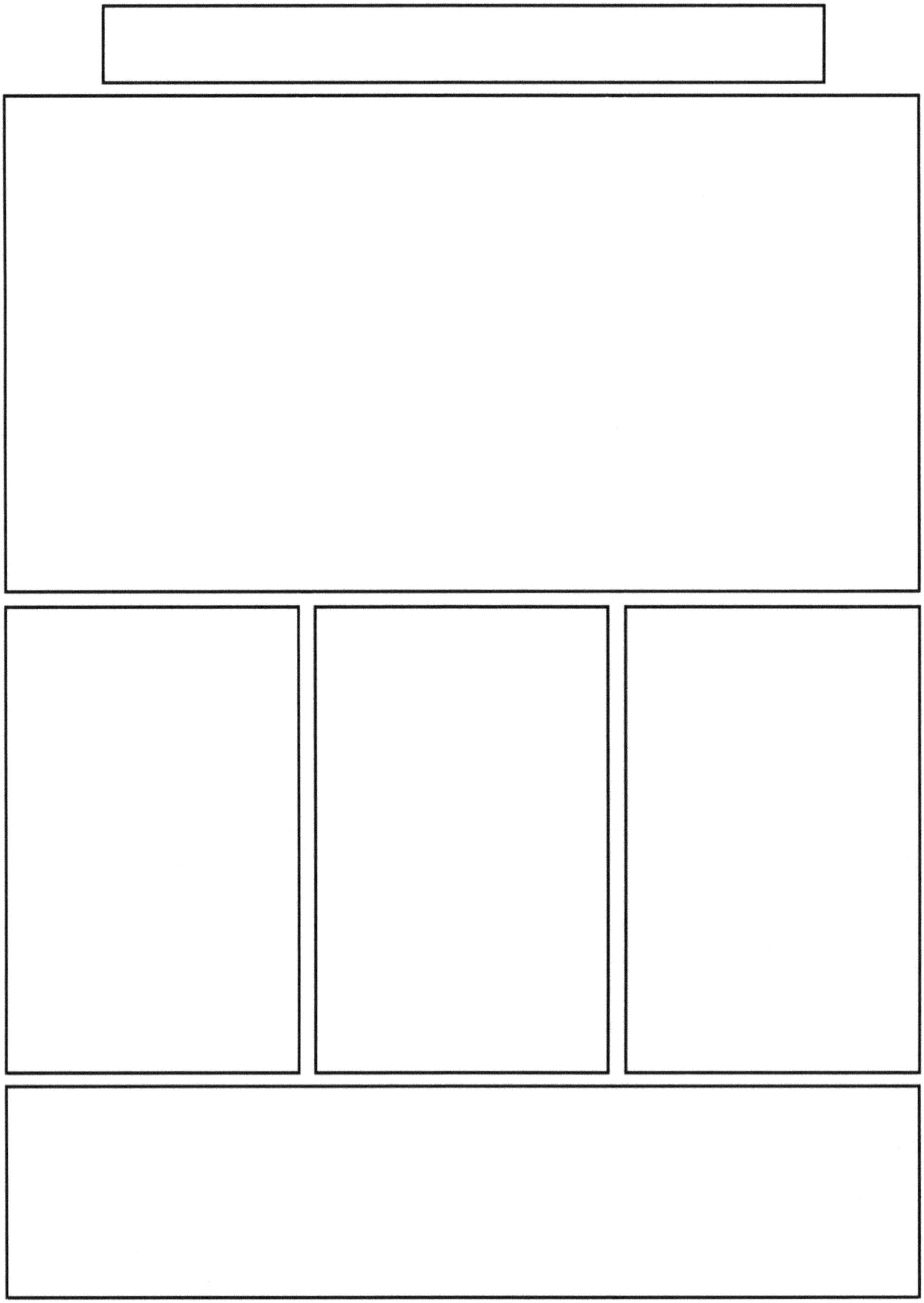

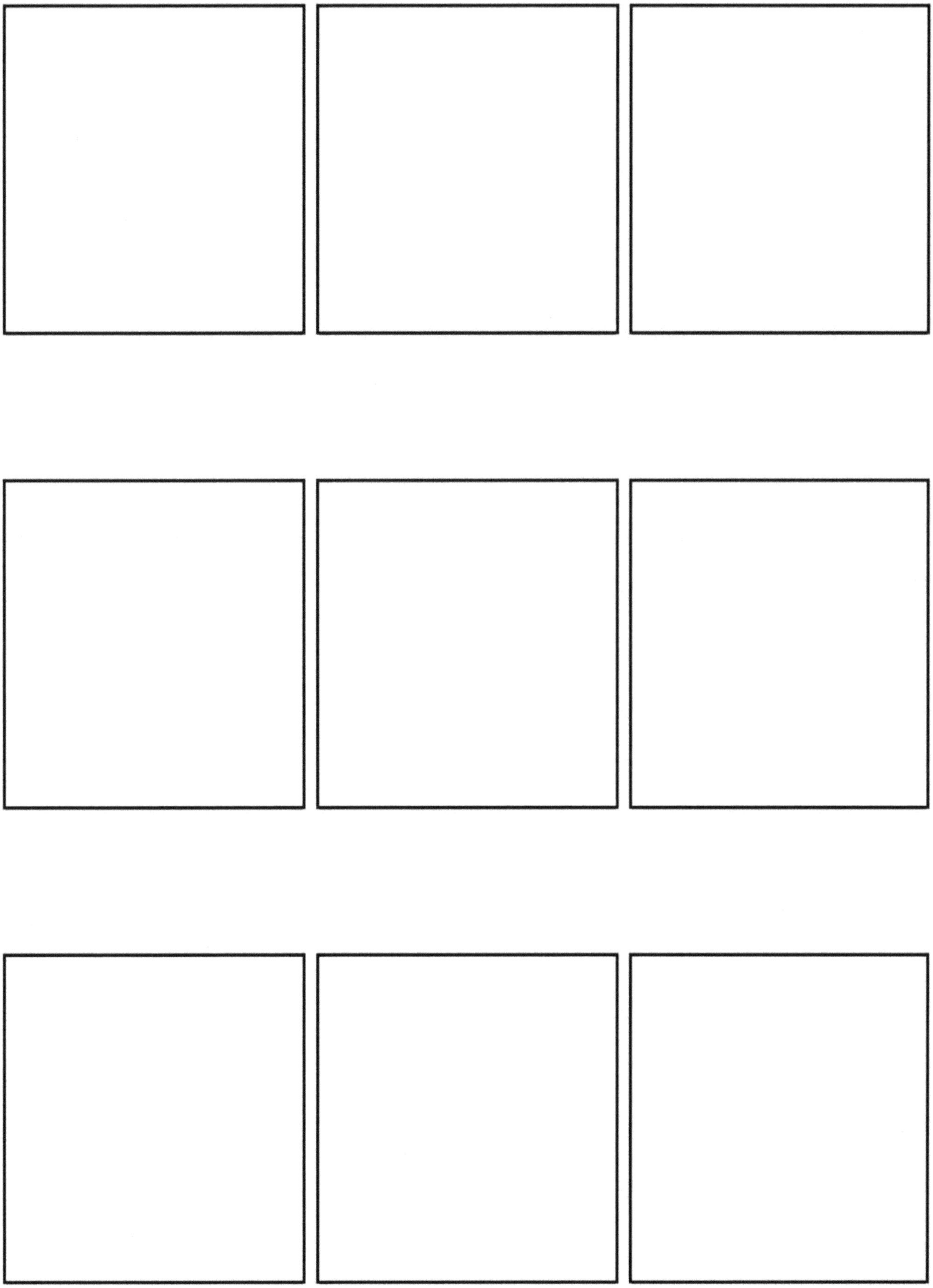

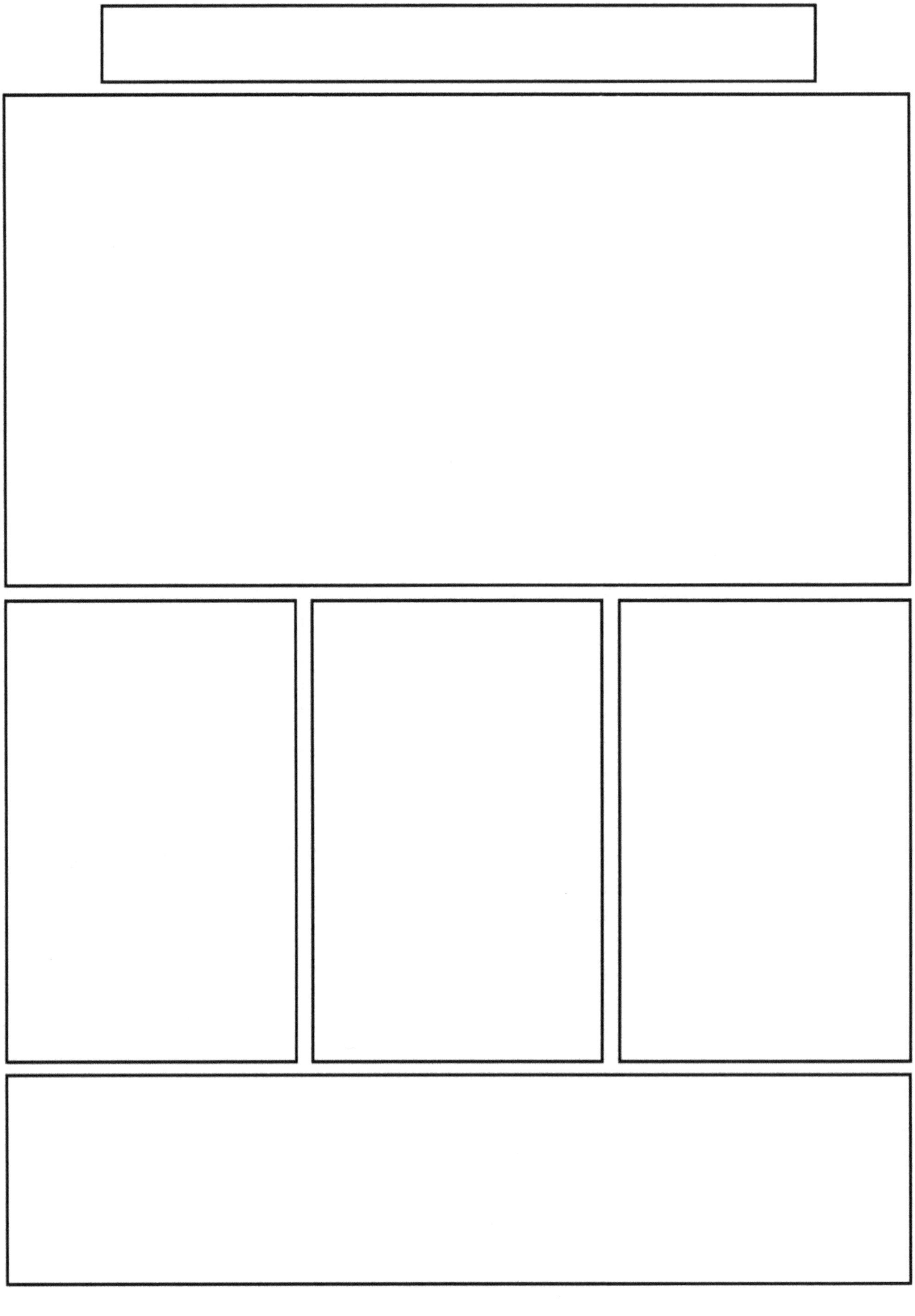

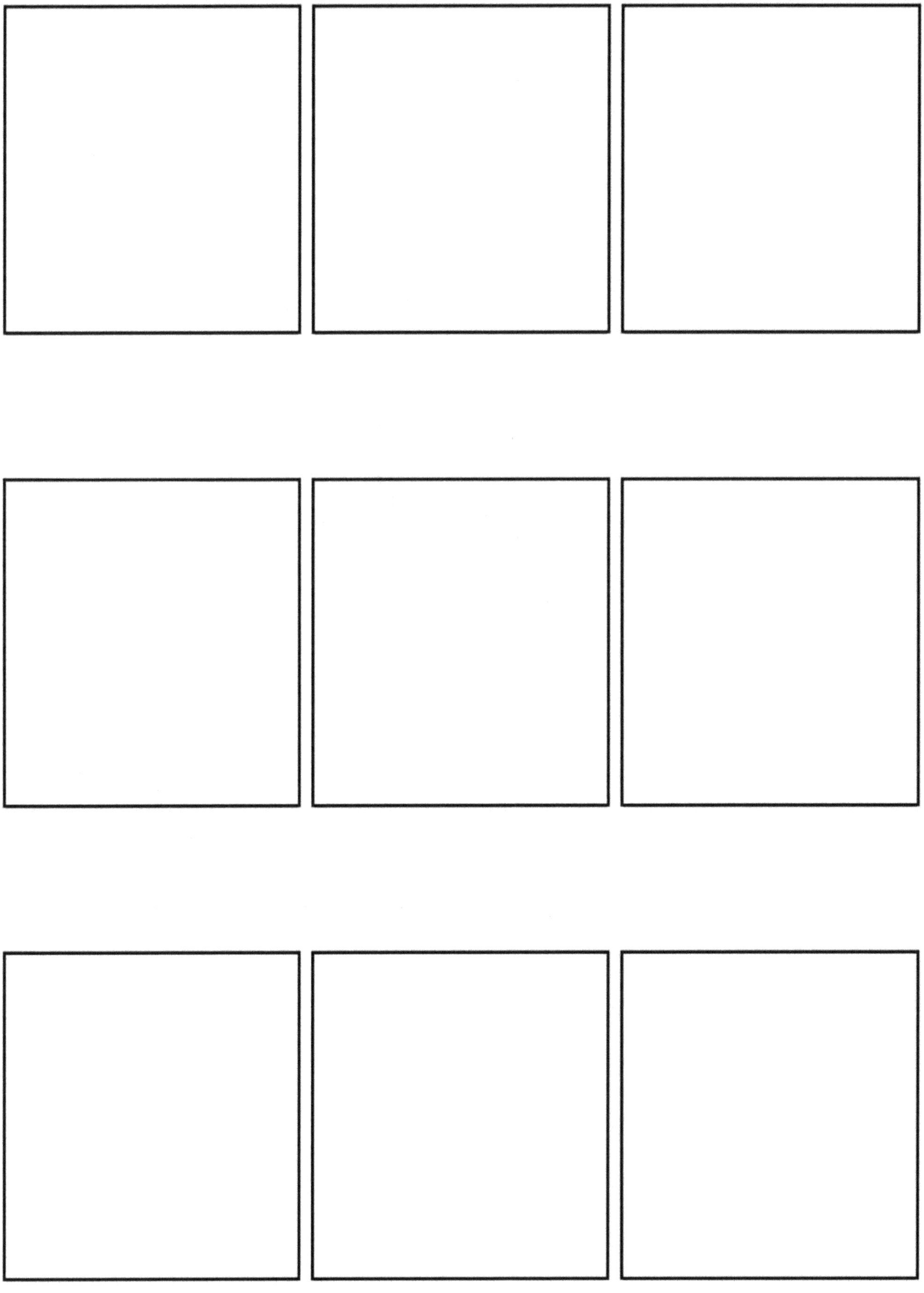

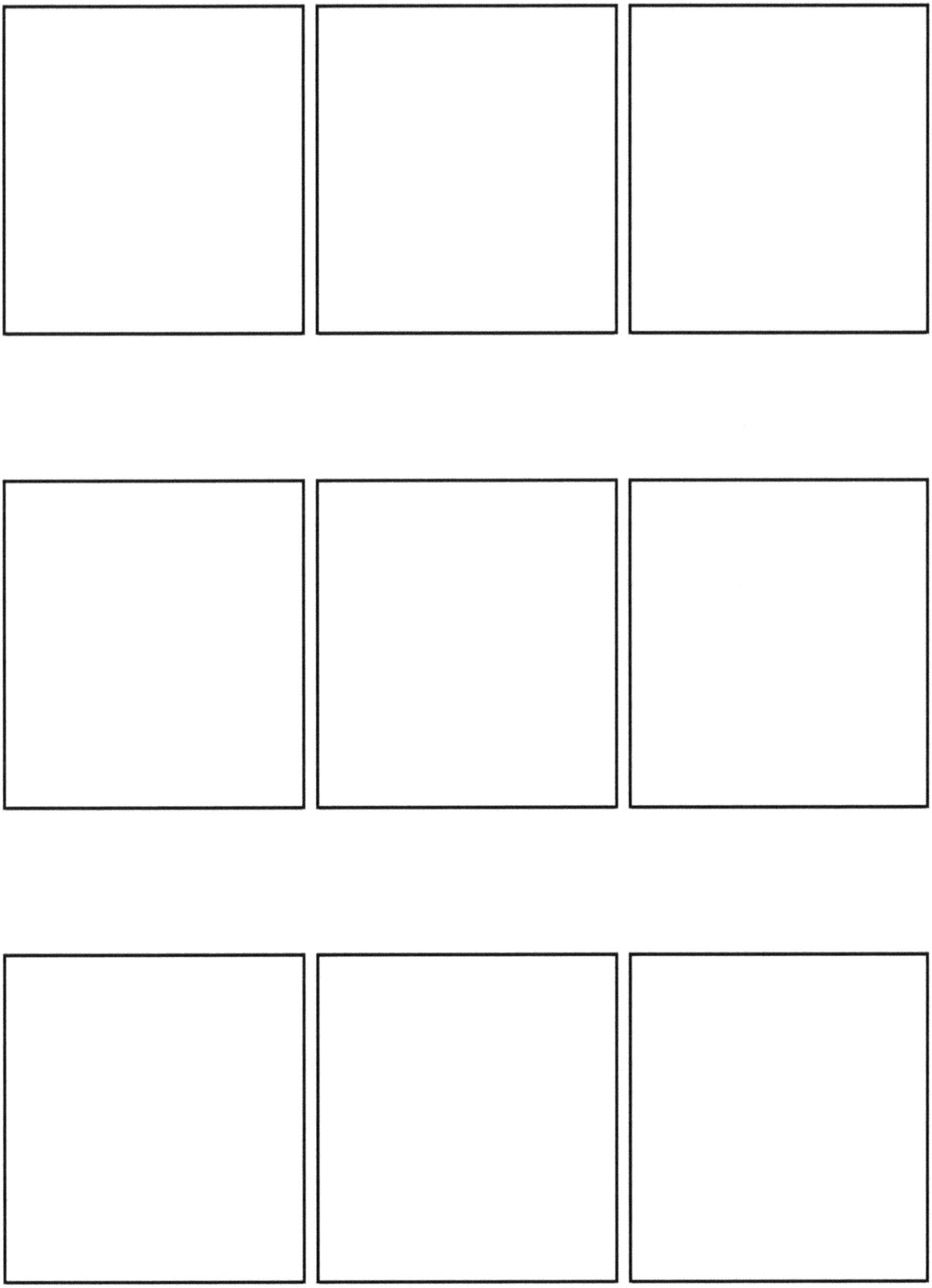

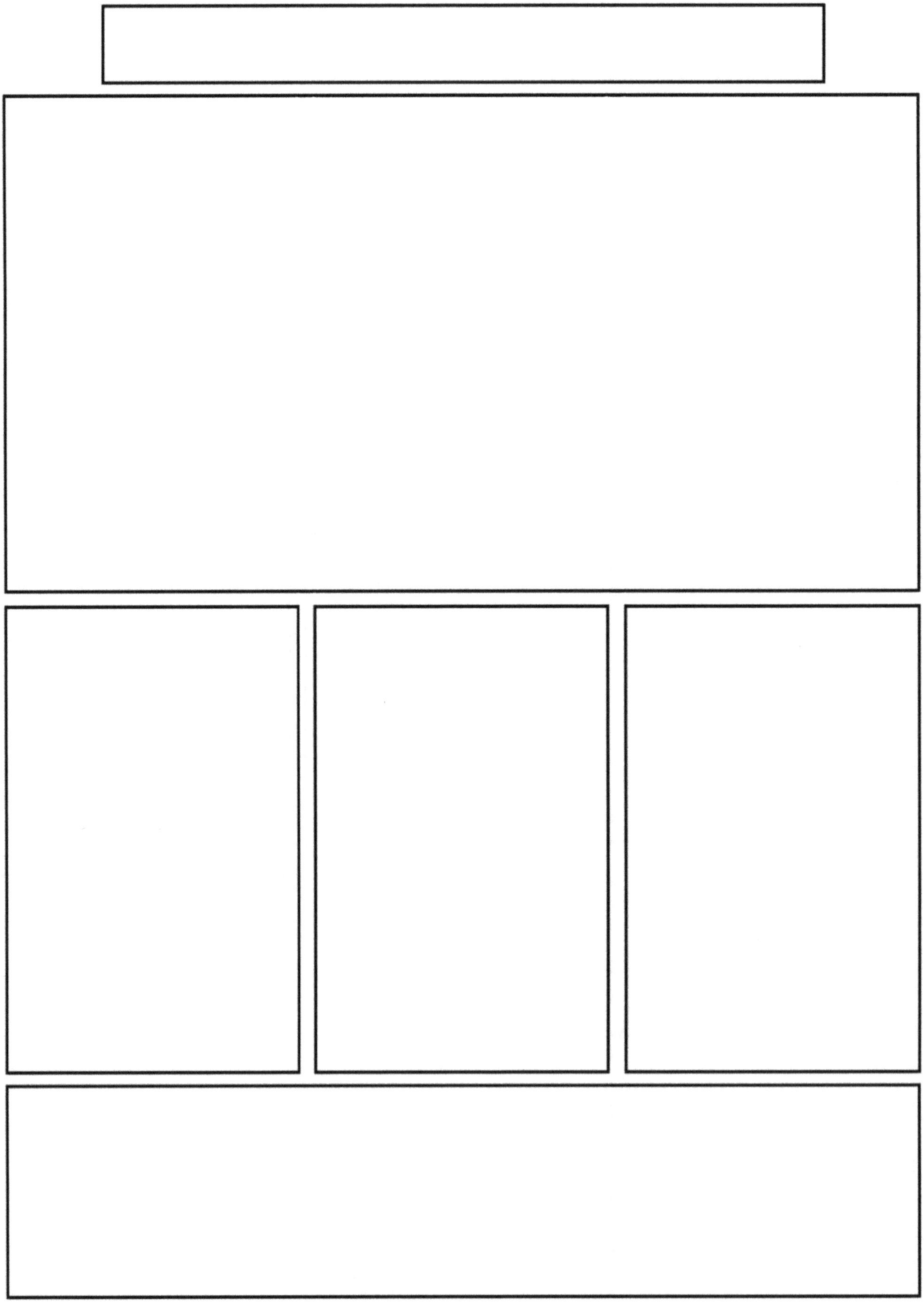

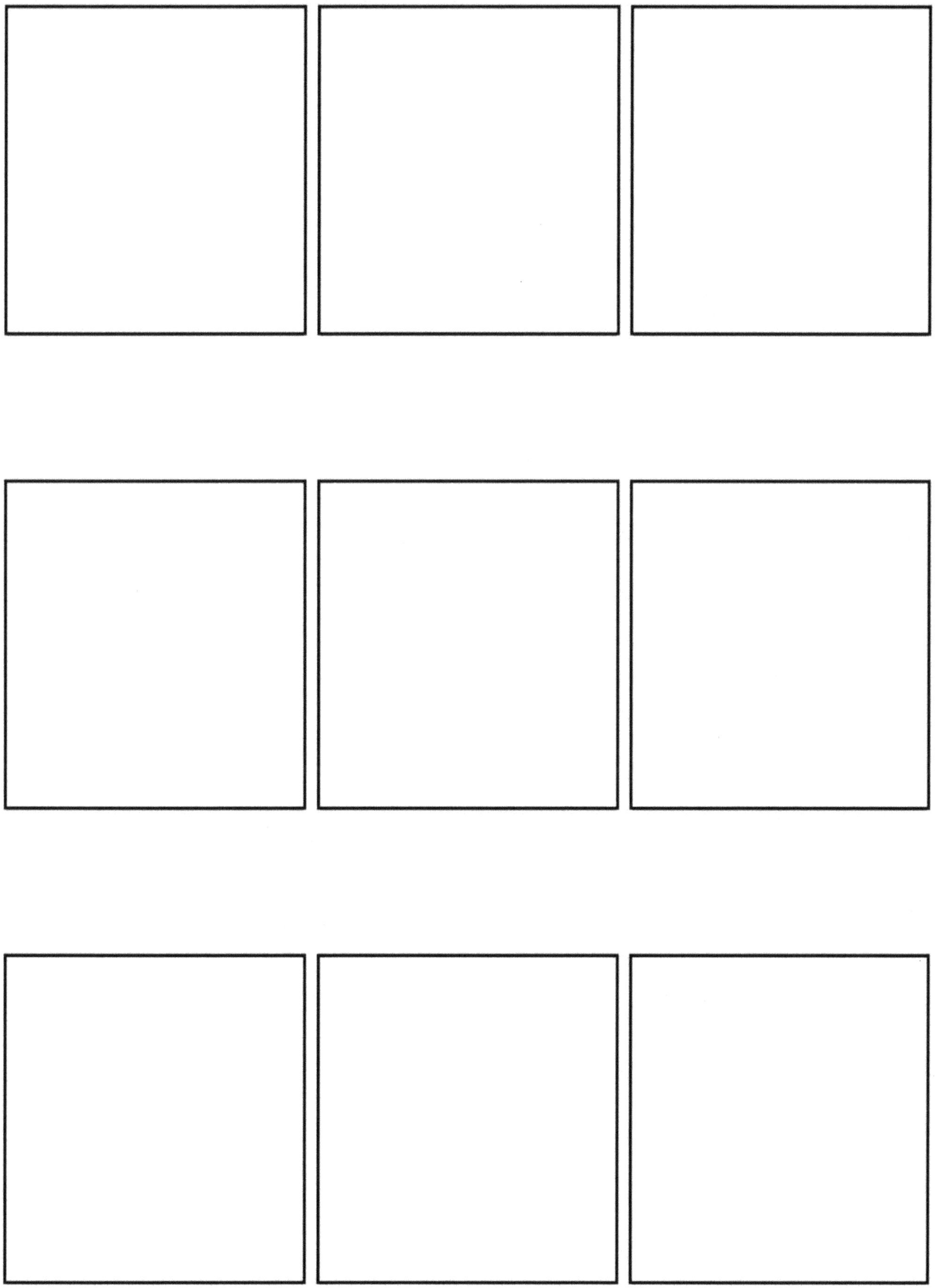

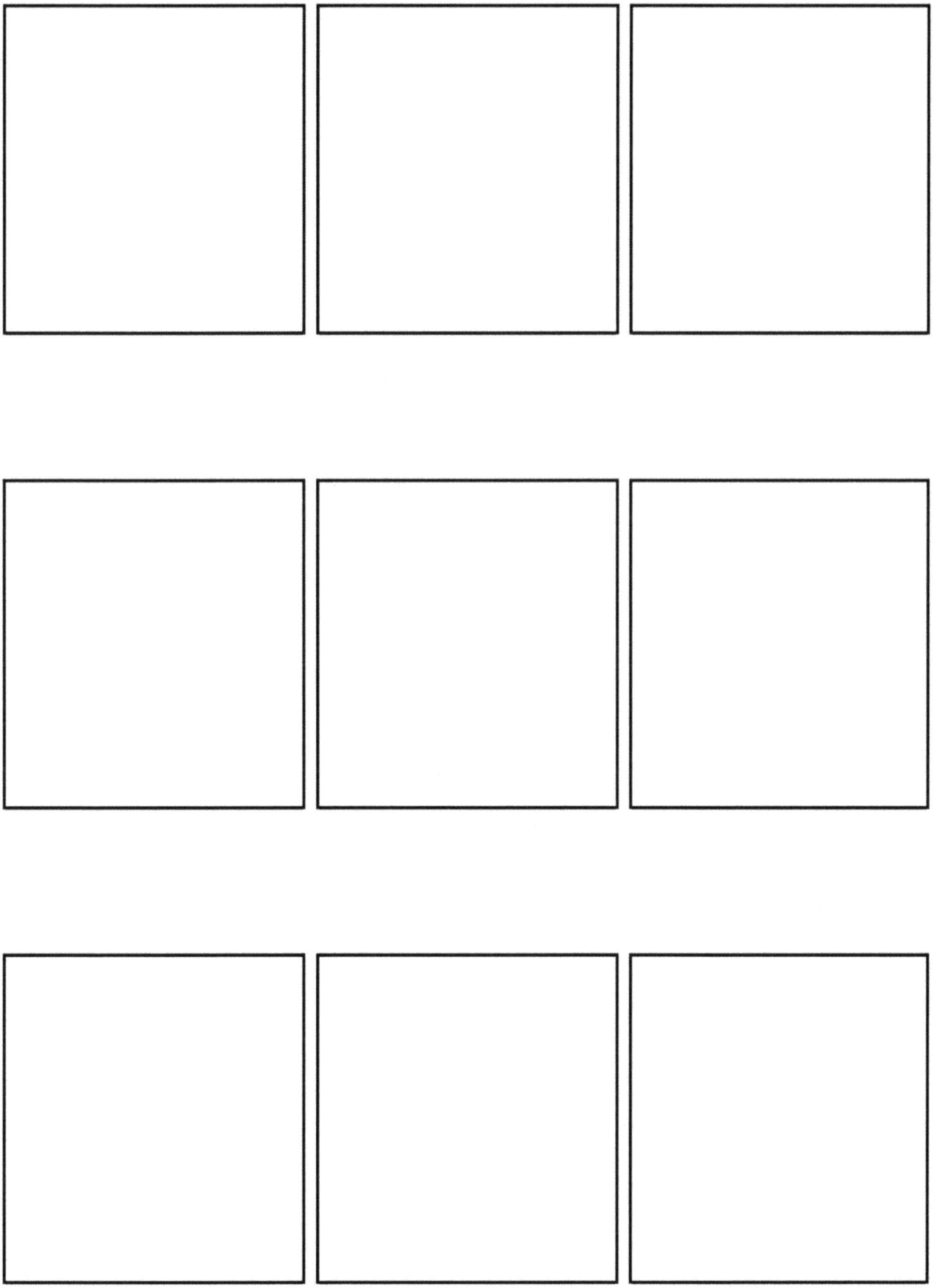

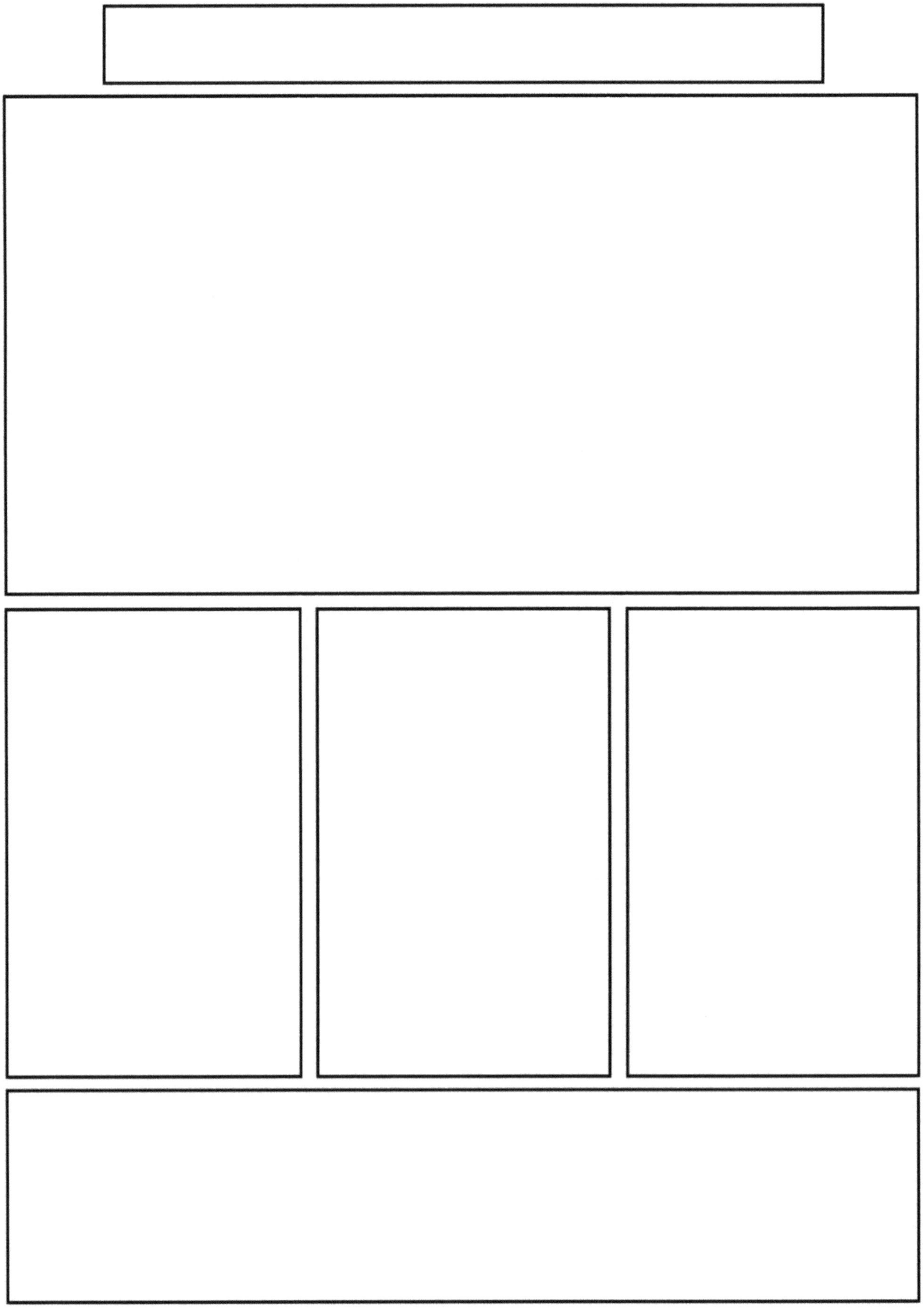

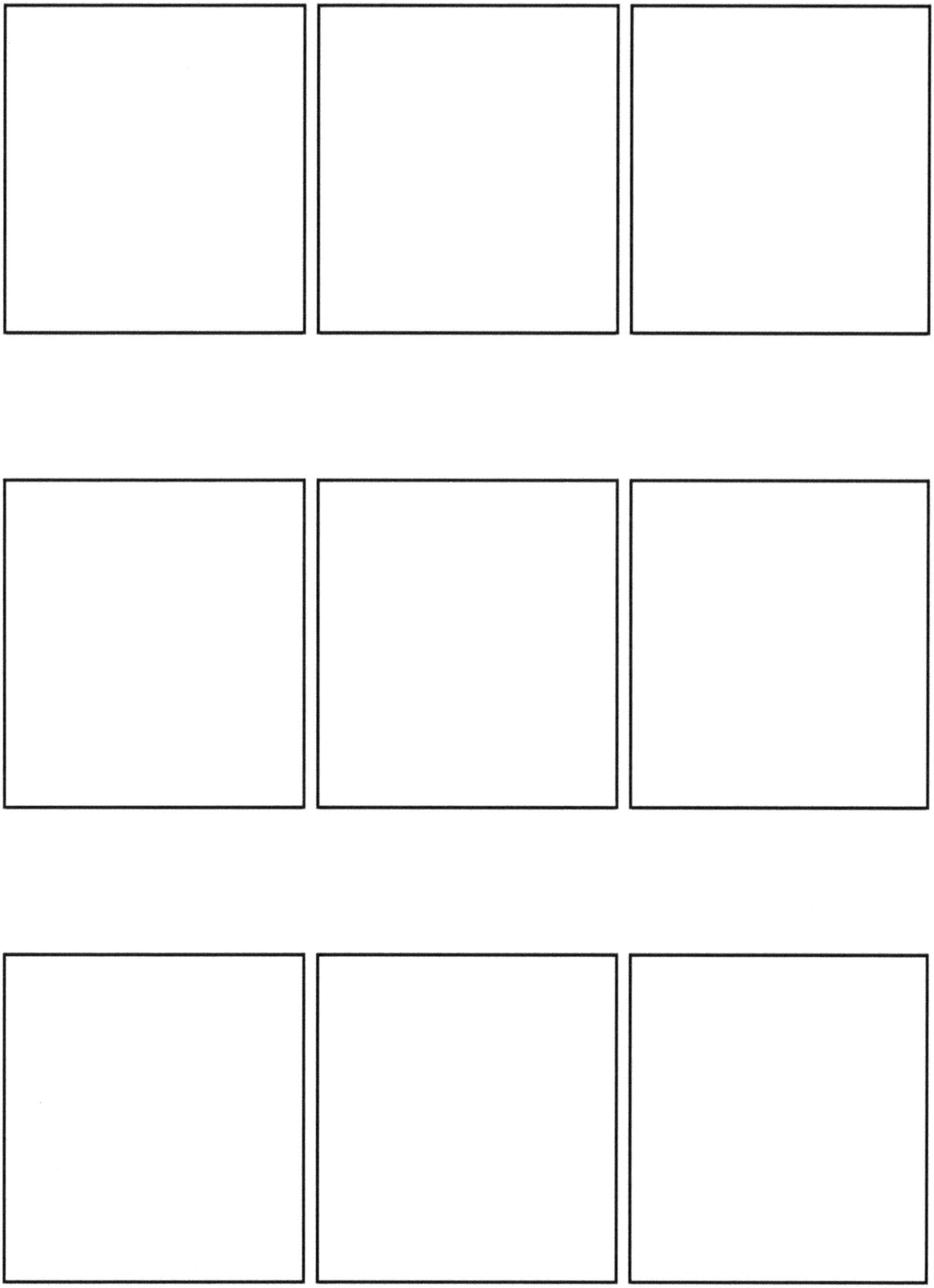

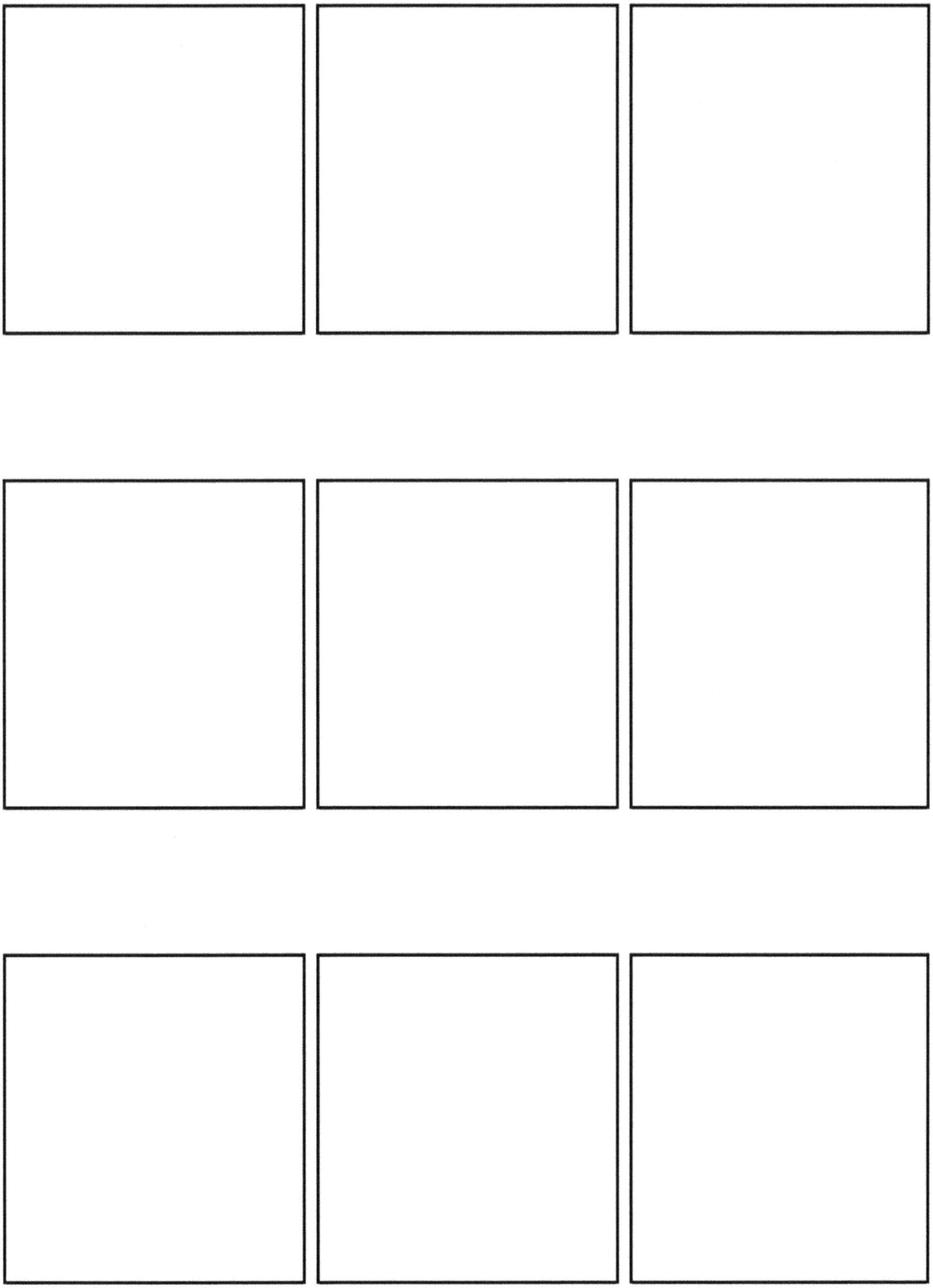

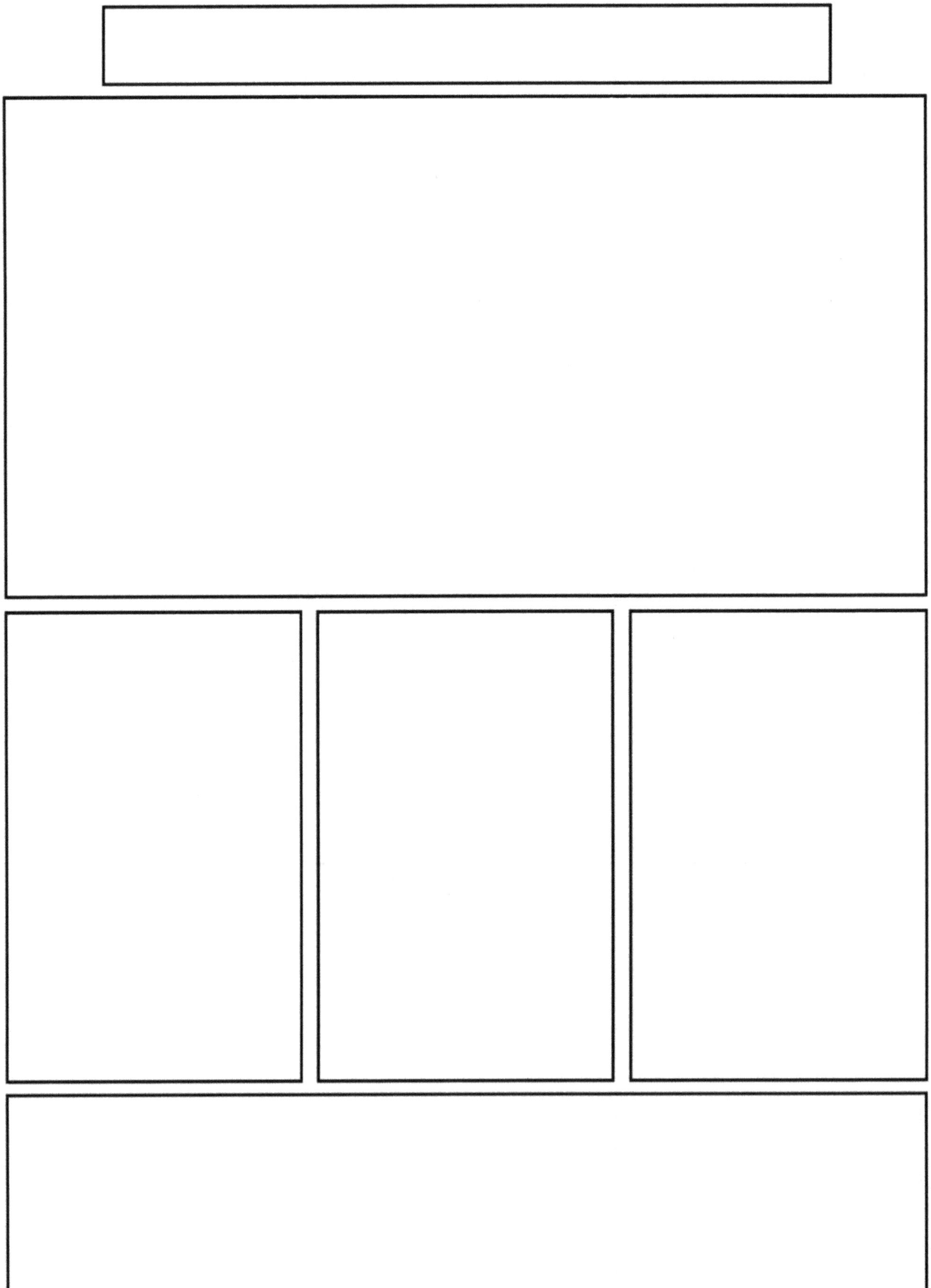

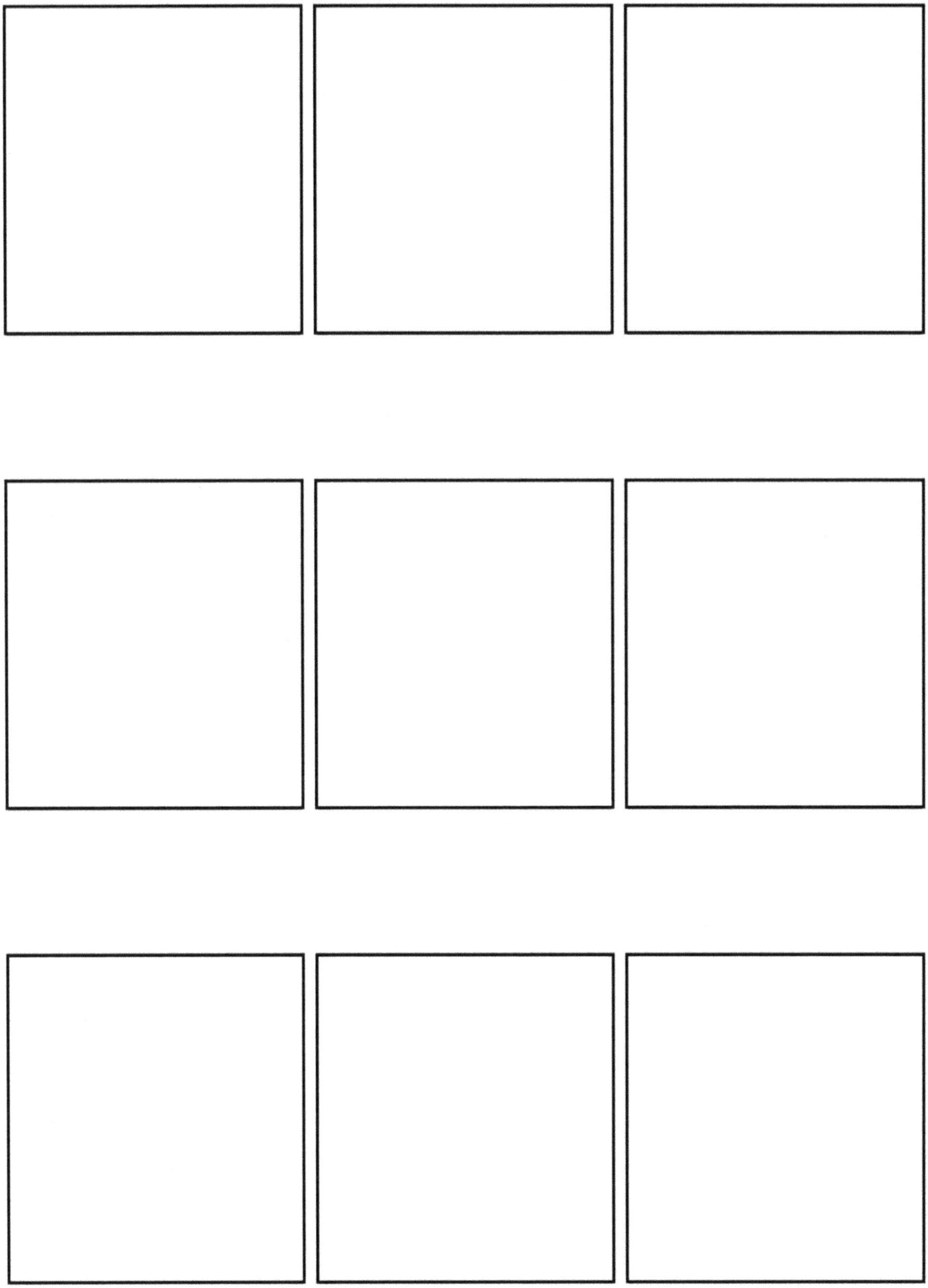

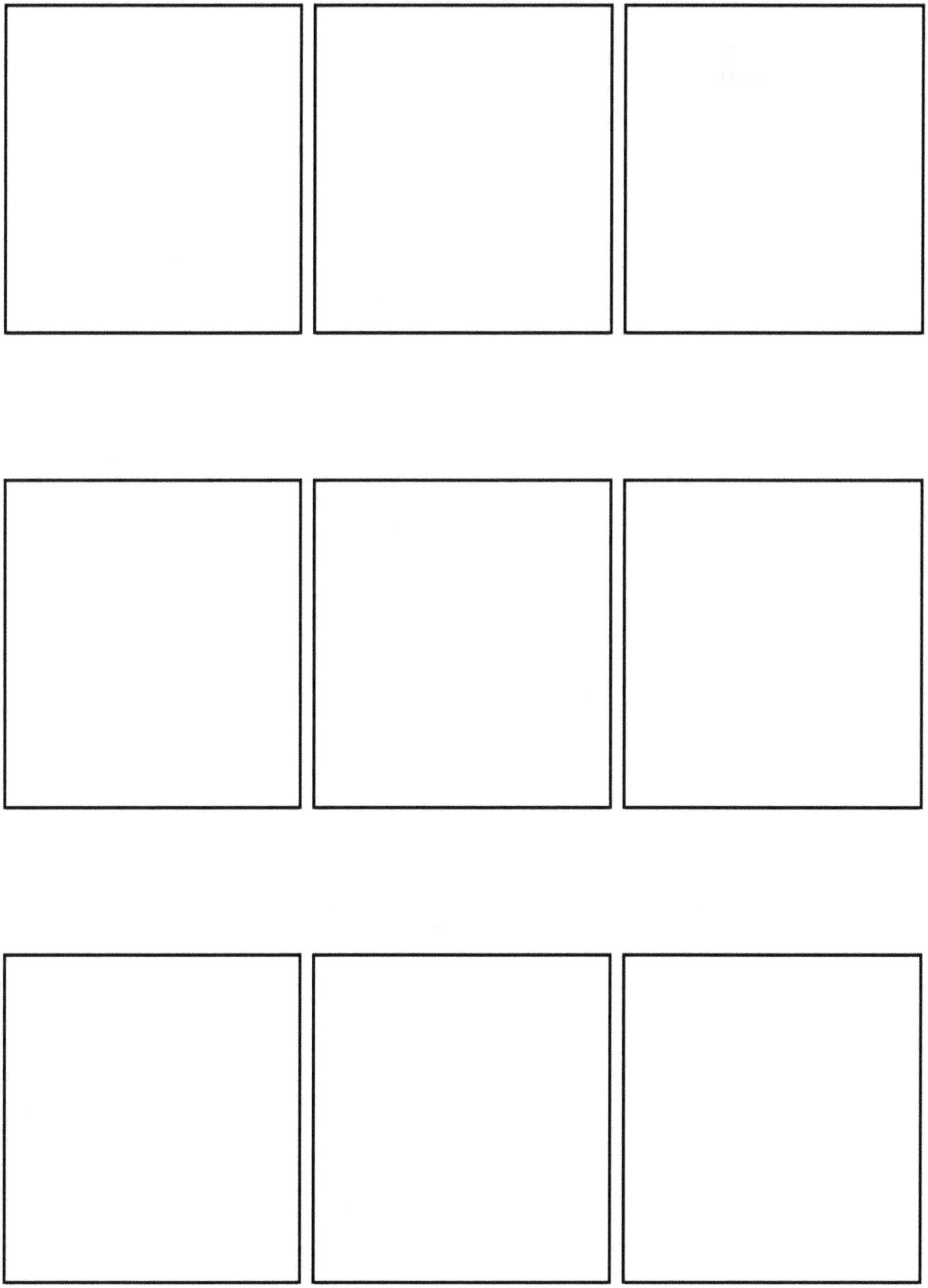

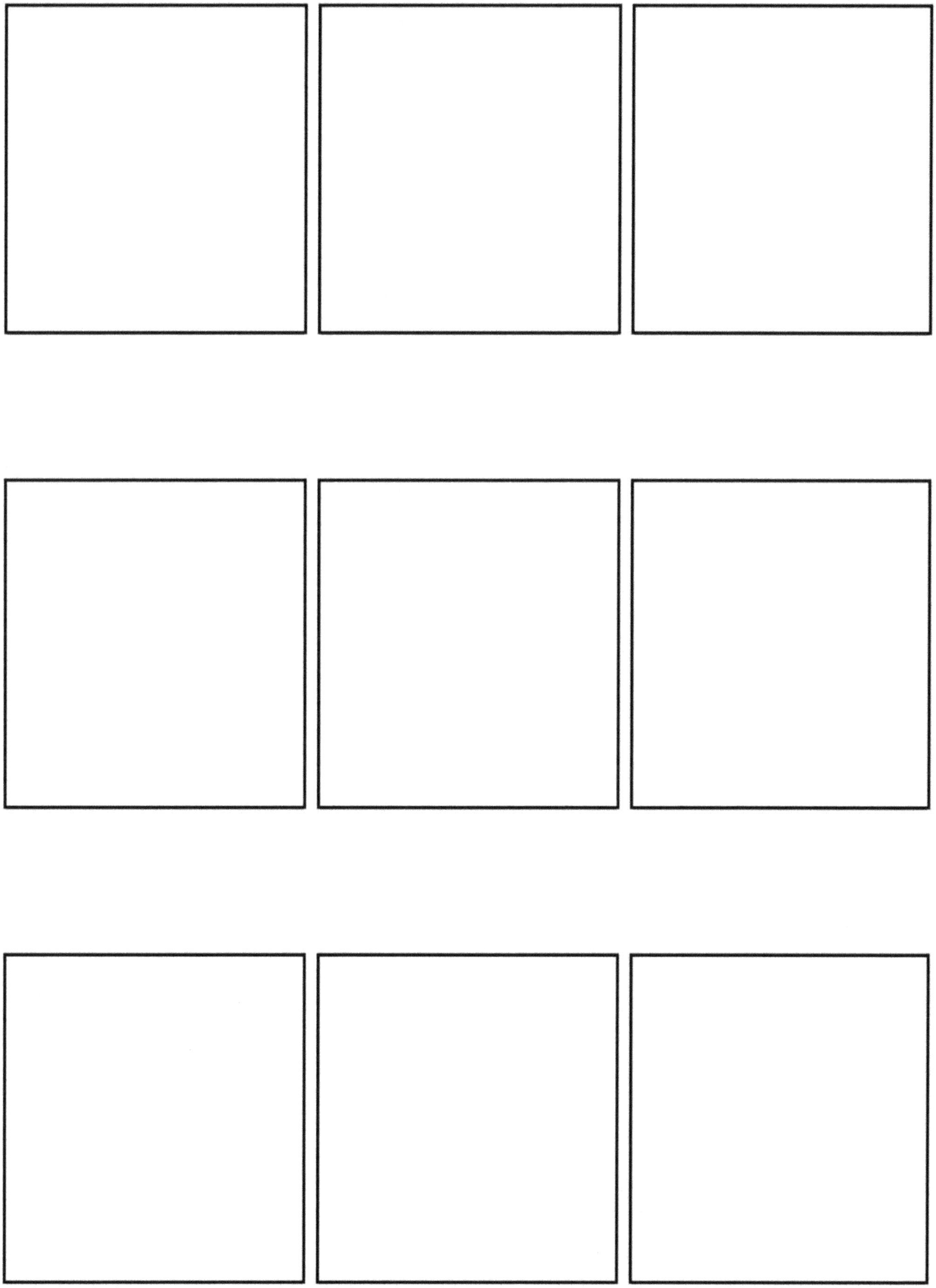

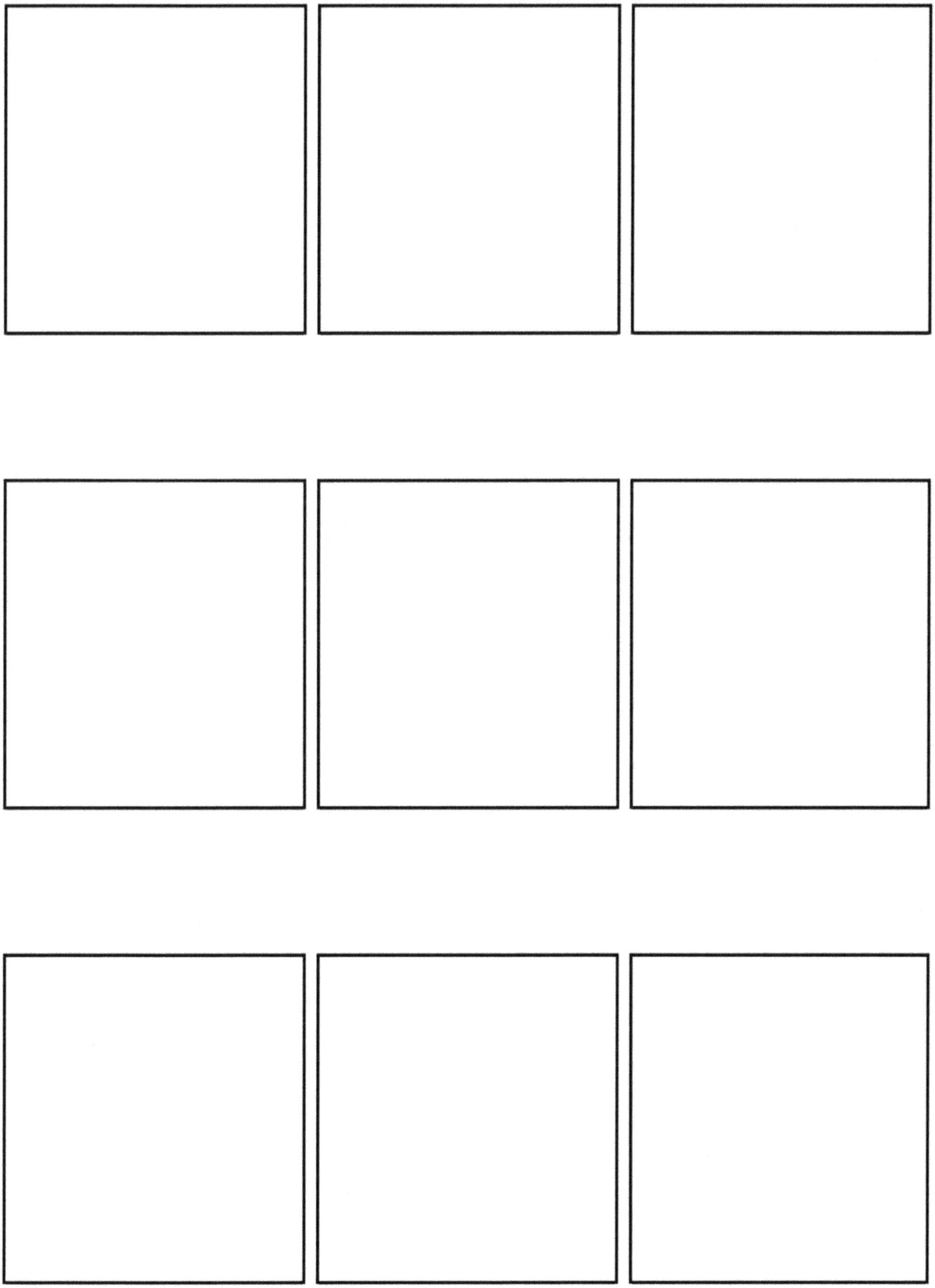

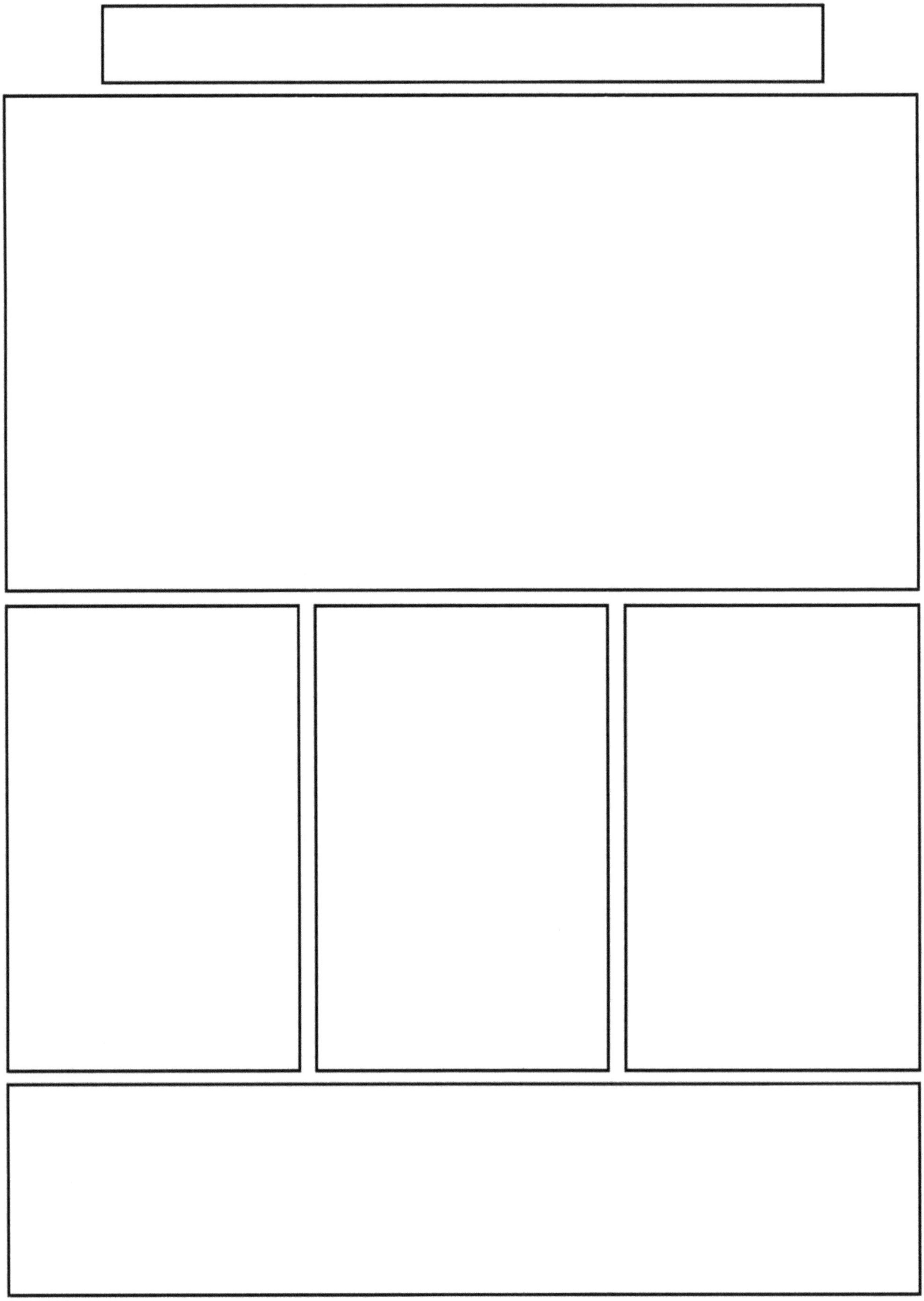

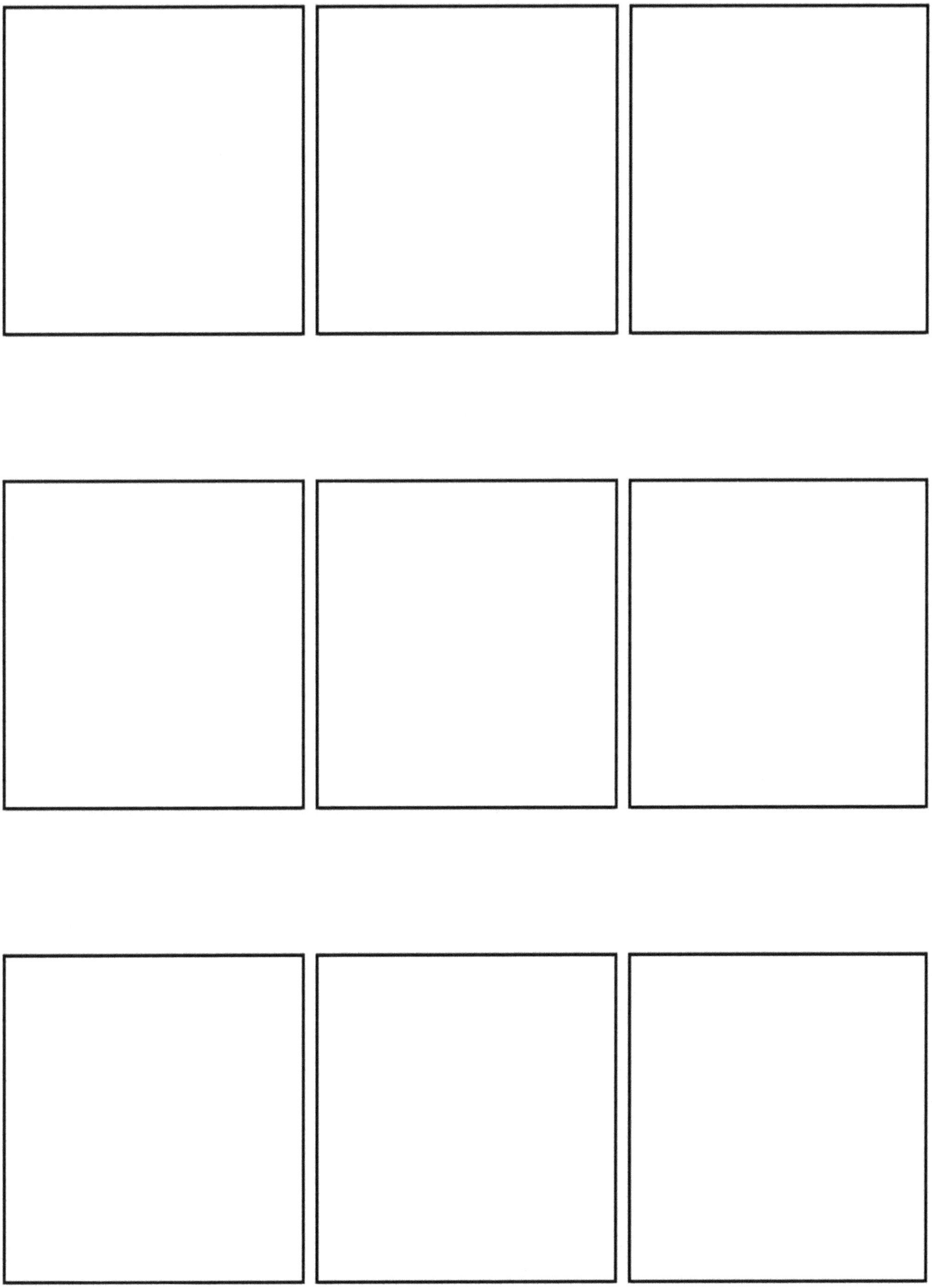

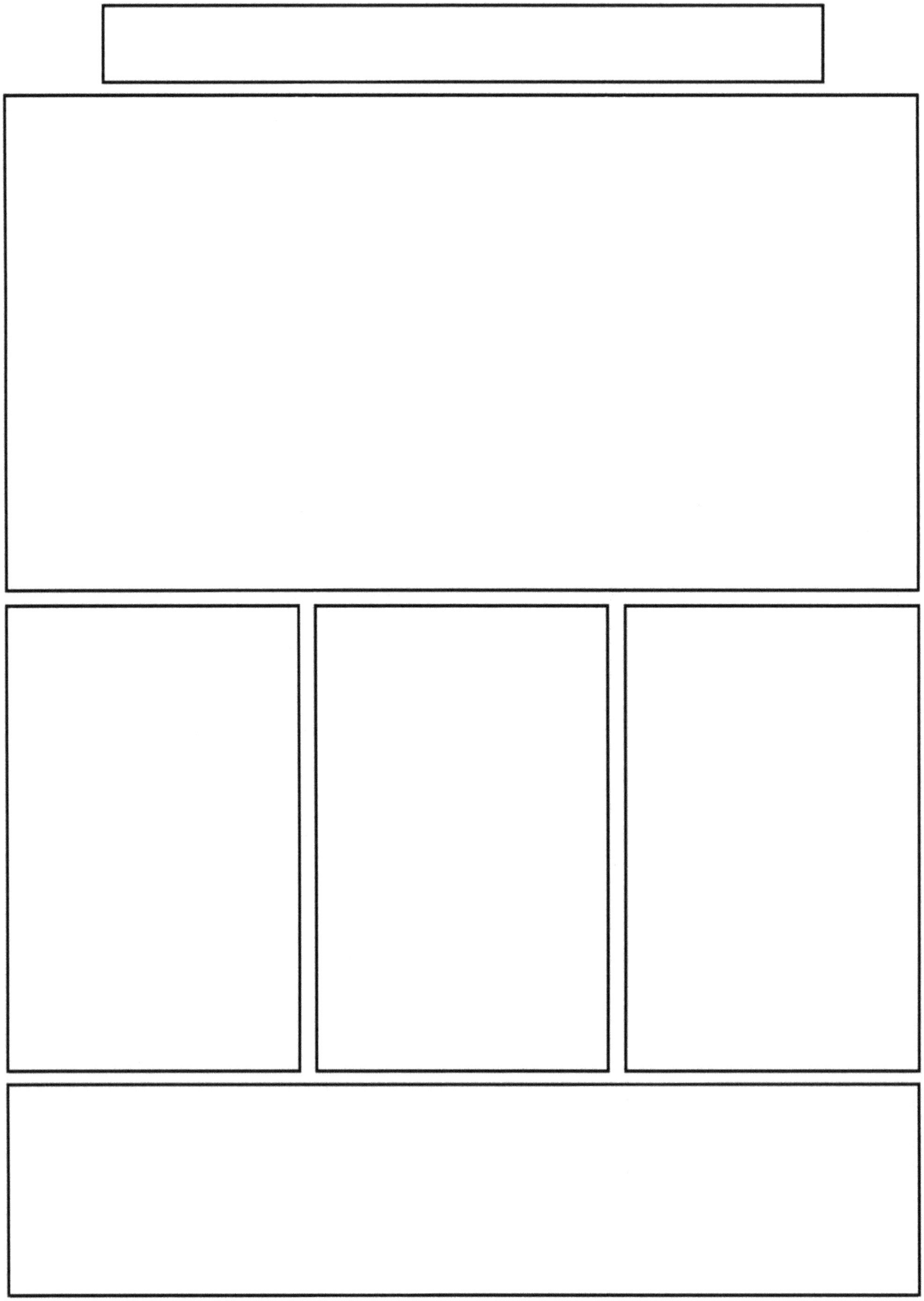

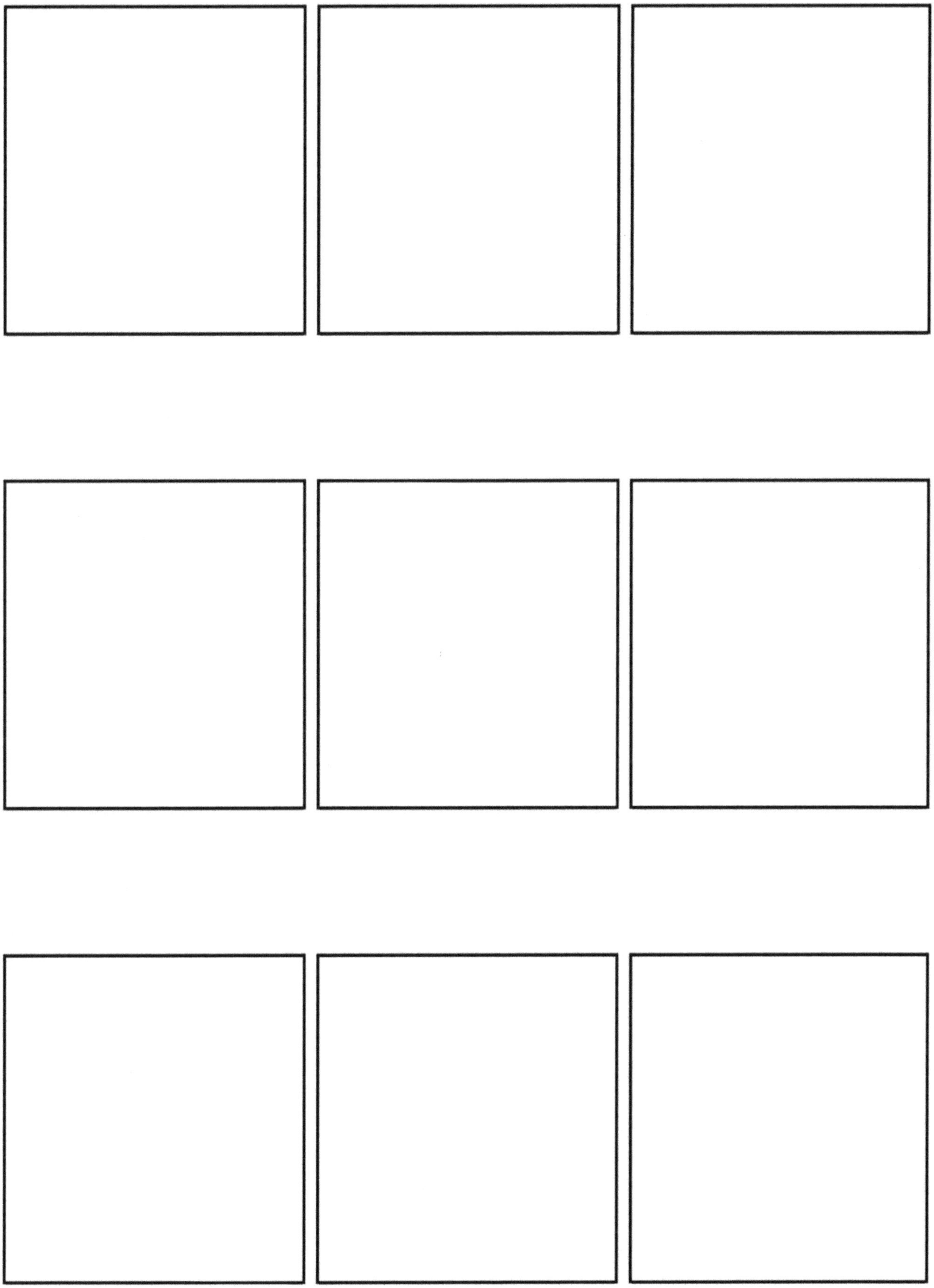

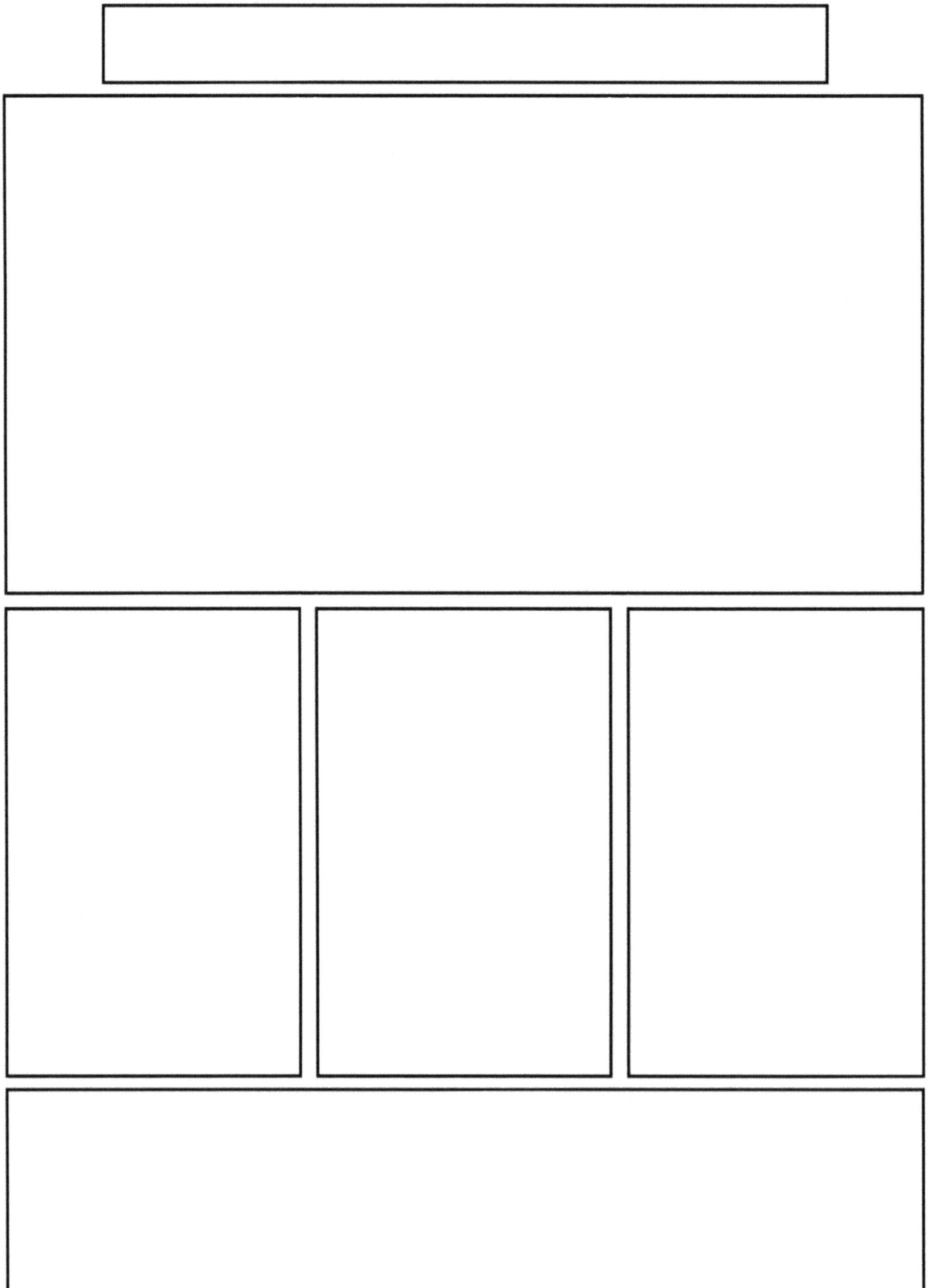

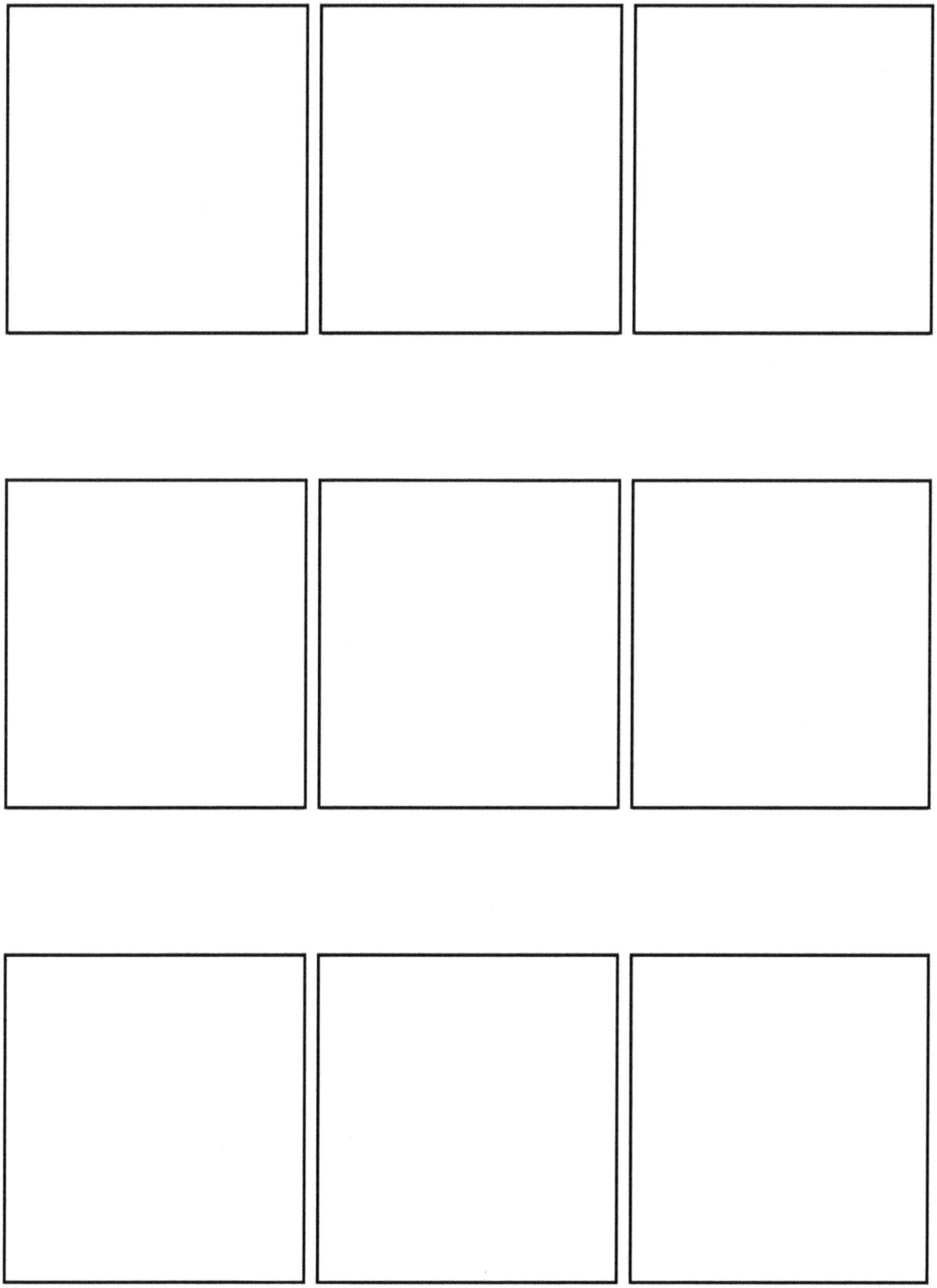

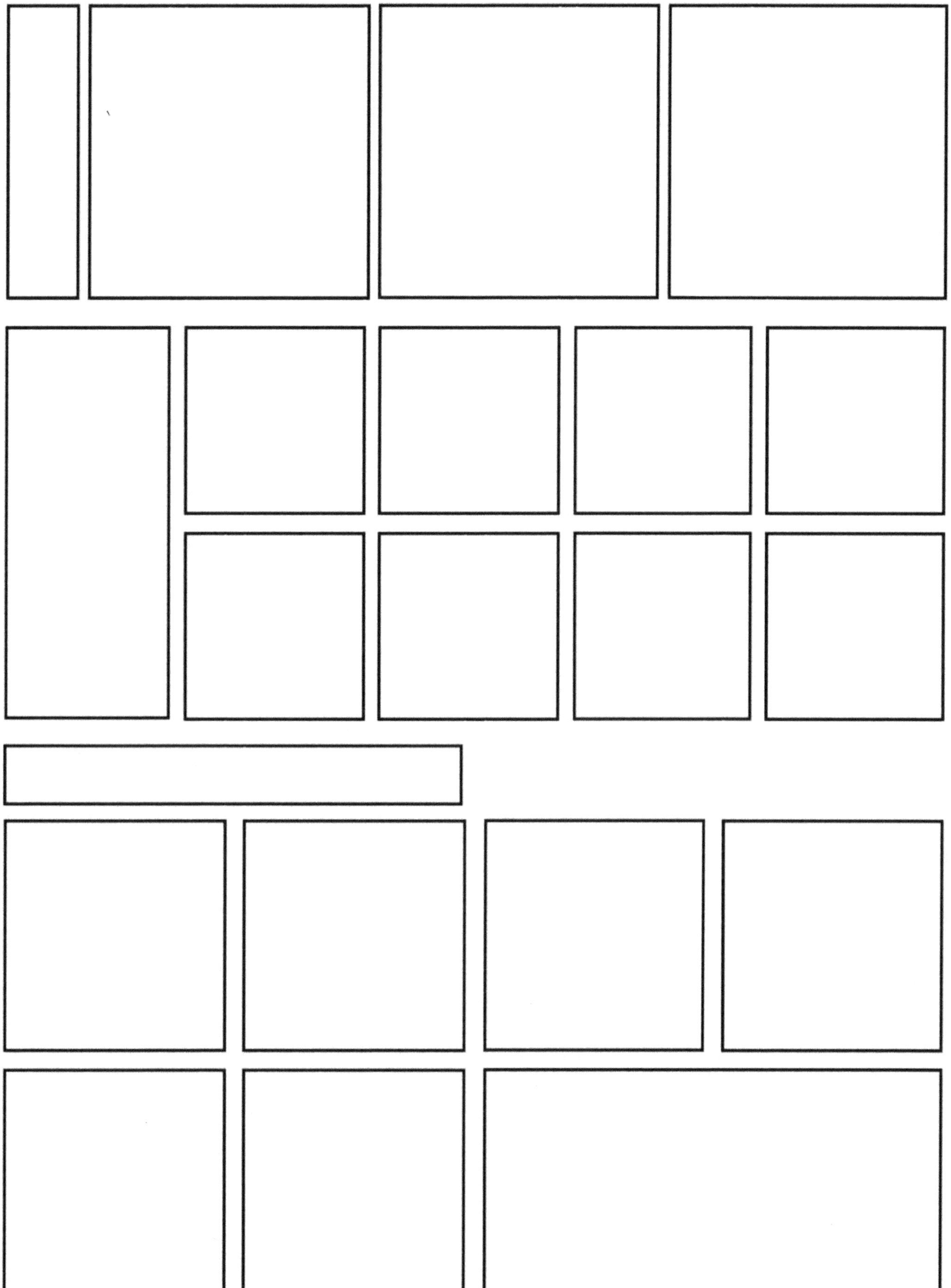

CPSIA information can be obtained
at www.ICGtesting.com
Printed in the USA
LVHW01s1116181217
560148LV00043B/2247/P

9 781978 448766